EXPOSING
THE SPIRITUAL FORCE BEHIND
RACIAL PREJUDICE

BY

CAROLYN PRISCILLA BYNUM

LIFE TO LEGACY

Exposing the Spiritual Force Behind Racial Prejudice

By: Carolyn Priscilla Bynum, Copyright © 2020

ISBN-13: 978-1-947288-57-7

Printed in the United States

10 9 8 7 6 5 4 3 2 1

Cover design by: Legacy Design Inc
                   Legacydesigninc@gmail.com

Published by: Life To Legacy, LLC
20650 S. Cicero Ave, #1239
Matteson, IL 60443
877-267-7477
Life2legacybooks@att.net

CONTENTS

ACKNOWLEDGMENTS

For all God's children throughout the entire earth.

FOREWORD

"But when it pleased God, who separated me from my mother's womb,
and called me by his grace, to reveal his Son in me, that I might preach
him among the heathen; immediately I conferred not with flesh and blood."
Galatians 1:15-16

Carolyn P. Bynum is a servant of God the Father, our Lord Jesus Christ, and my wife also. She is a pastor, teacher, and songwriter of the Lord, and the best gift God could give to a man. I am proud and honored to be her husband of 43 years. We have two sons and four granddaughters.

Pastor Carolyn, as we all refer to her in Restoration Christian Ministries Center, has always served the Lord with her beautiful and anointed voice, but now with the sharing of the Gospel (Good News) for nearly 25 years. With the Lord's anointed teaching, she has set many captives free, healed the sick, and brought knowledge to many by the Spirit of the Word, starting with me.

Pastor Carolyn has the respect of many sons of God with me being the first. She has my support in all that she does and wants to do forever. It is my pleasure and honor to serve the Lord with her in ministry.

Forever together in spirit and love!

—Bishop Paul E. Bynum, Sr.

INTRODUCTION

RACIAL PREJUDICE IS MAGNIFIED TODAY MORE THAN EVER DESPITE generations of outcries for justice for all. From its origin, to slavery, to the subtle slights in everyday interactions, this monster is never satiated. Perpetuated by fear, ignorance, and hatred, it breathes out the fire of its rage in acts of heinous violence inflicting lifelong scars physically, emotionally, socially, economically, and spiritually, on all in its path. Its long-term effect is humanly impossible to calculate.

One may go back generations upon generations and find the same monstrous effect. Its method of operating is the same, yet few have figured out the why of it all. The entire space of this book can be used to recall countless examples of racial injustice; however, that is not its purpose. We all know there is a problem, but we all do not know that there is truly an answer. A life-changing, world-changing answer! An answer that is foolproof that would bring lasting positive change if people only understood the spiritual influence behind racism and how it manages to transcend generations.

At the time of this writing, there is tremendous unrest and racial prejudice is again at the center. Coupled with a pandemic that is ravaging the world, which should bring people together instead of driving them apart, the state-of-affairs for many is one of hopelessness. For complete accuracy of the present state, we will go ahead and squeeze in the economic collapse also. There are other simultaneous calamities but at some point, we must begin to bring the answer into focus. What a mess indeed, yet the Answer has handled it all. Note the past tense.

Racial prejudice, one of many prejudices, will continue to permeate every area of life, tarnish and cripple every generation, and slither unscathed at will until a clear understanding of the spiritual force behind it is grasped and replaced with that which is just. Without discernment, no man, group, or system will ever be able to uproot this evil. Attempting to acknowledge the psychology of it all has little or no practical relevance because of its danger and desperation cries out for the immediacy of change.

A fallen nature is at work that is stronger than any human being's ability without the Power of God's inworking. Neither natural position, power, intelligence nor ability enter the equation here. However, a spiritual view of Ezekiel 28:1-19, by God's Spirit, will make an open show of what is stealthily at work behind this evil. May the wisdom of God accompany the reader through the following pages of insight.

CHAPTER 1

UNMASKING THE LAWLESS ONE

This is my commandment, that ye love one another, as I have loved you.

John 15:12

FROM THE BIBLE ONE CAN SEE THERE WAS A GREAT BREACH BETWEEN God and man in the Book of Genesis. The ramifications of that breach have reverberated throughout the history of mankind and are on course to continue unhindered until mankind submits wholeheartedly to God's Remedy. It all began in Eden with a man called Adam along with his wife, Eve. A new view with a precise focus of what truly was lost is buried in the Book of Ezekiel, Chapter 28:1-19 (KJV). Man has been trying to recoup what was lost in Eden on his own ever since.

Once the Holy Spirit unveils His meaning when He inspired Ezekiel to write, the lawless one will be stripped completely with no heart or mind to hide in ever again. Ezekiel's prophecy is fulfilled in Christ Jesus; therefore, the reader is encouraged to read the following verses from the perspective of a Finished Work and let our mission begin.

SCRIPTURE READING

1 The word of the LORD came again unto me, saying, 2 Son of man, say unto the prince of Tyrus, Thus saith the Lord GOD; Because thine heart is lifted up, and thou hast said, I am a God, I sit in the seat of God, in the midst of the seas; yet thou art a man,

and not God, though thou set thine heart as the heart of God: 3 Behold, thou art wiser than Daniel; there is no secret that they can hide from thee: 4 With thy wisdom and with thine understanding thou hast gotten thee riches, and hast gotten gold and silver into thy treasures: 5 By thy great wisdom and by thy traffick hast thou increased thy riches, and thine heart is lifted up because of thy riches: 6 Therefore thus saith the Lord GOD; Because thou hast set thine heart as the heart of God; 7 Behold, therefore I will bring strangers upon thee, the terrible of the nations: and they shall draw their swords against the beauty of thy wisdom, and they shall defile thy brightness. 8 They shall bring thee down to the pit, and thou shalt die the deaths of them that are slain in the midst of the seas. 9 Wilt thou yet say before him that slayeth thee, I am God? but thou shalt be a man, and no God, in the hand of him that slayeth thee. 10 Thou shalt die the deaths of the uncircumcised by the hand of strangers: for I have spoken it, saith the Lord GOD. 11 Moreover the word of the LORD came unto me, saying, 12 Son of man, take up a lamentation upon the king of Tyrus, and say unto him, Thus saith the Lord GOD; Thou sealest up the sum, full of wisdom, and perfect in beauty. 13 Thou hast been in Eden the garden of God; every precious stone was thy covering, the sardius, topaz, and the diamond, the beryl, the onyx, and the jasper, the sapphire, the emerald, and the carbuncle, and gold: the workmanship of thy tabrets and of thy pipes was prepared in thee in the day that thou wast created. 14 Thou art the anointed cherub that covereth; and I have set thee so: thou wast upon the holy mountain of God; thou hast walked up and down in the midst of the stones of fire. 15 Thou wast perfect in thy ways from the day that thou wast created, till iniquity was found in thee. 16 By the multitude of thy merchandise they have filled the midst of thee with violence, and thou hast sinned: therefore I will cast thee as profane out of the mountain of God: and I will destroy thee, O covering cherub, from the midst of the stones of fire. 17 Thine heart was lifted up because of thy beauty, thou hast corrupted thy wisdom by reason of thy brightness: I will cast thee to the ground, I will lay thee before kings, that they may behold thee. 18 Thou hast defiled thy sanctuaries by the multitude of thine iniquities, by the iniquity of thy traffick; therefore will I bring forth a fire from the midst of thee, it shall devour thee, and I will bring thee to ashes upon the earth in the sight of all them that behold thee. 19 All they that know thee among the people shall be astonished at thee: thou shalt be a terror, and never shalt thou be any more.   Ezekiel 28:1-19, KJV

Then Peter opened his mouth, and said, Of a truth I perceive that God is no respecter of persons:

But in every nation he that feareth him, and worketh righteousness, is accepted with him.

Acts 10:34-35

CHAPTER 2

IT ALL BEGAN IN THE HEART

SURELY, THE READER WILL HAVE NOTED THAT THE VERSES ABOVE DEAL with the prince of Tyrus and may wonder what he has to do with Adam or us today. Everything! The force of sin was unleashed in the disobedience of Adam. His "trademark" is seen in all the subsequent accounts of disobedience toward God in Scripture. Romans 5:19 helps with this point which reads, "For as by one man's disobedience many were made sinners, so by the obedience of one shall many be made righteous." Remember it!

The Adamic influence gets more pronounced as Ezekiel, Chapter 28:1-19 is developed. The breach is immediately set forth in the first two verses where it states the man's heart was exalted so that in his own eyes, he usurped the place and power of God. To whom is he accountable? Nobody but himself! After all, he believes he is God. Although he set his heart as that of God, God reminded him that he was a mere man.

It is always blatantly evident when a man's heart is exalted against God in this manner. He becomes more lawless, controlling, and reckless by the moment and many choose to overlook gross misdeeds and further enable his ego, robotically yielding to him as though he is God. The emission of fear is inherent in his wicked spirit.

There are numerous examples of Scripture where the heart of one is exalted against God. God warns of the effect of such a move many times in the Old Testament. For instance, King Uzziah looms large. This king amassed a great host, superior weaponry and built towers. He was famous abroad and according to the Bible (2 Chronicles 26:15), was marvelously helped until he was strong. The natural strength or pride of life is a peak at which a downward spiral commences for many. It is there the heart is often lifted up against God, and the rogue blindly goes on his own to the peril of many.

2 Chronicles 26:16, plots the next step for our learning. "But when he was strong, his heart was lifted up to his destruction: for he transgressed against the LORD his God and went into the temple of the LORD to burn incense upon the altar of incense." What a trespass! Uzziah usurped the office of the priesthood. No limits in his heart despite God's commands. Totally disregarding the intervention of God's true priests, Uzziah stubbornly proceeded and leprosy rose up in his forehead before the priests in the house of the LORD from beside the incense altar.

Amazingly, in the year King Uzziah died the prophet Isaiah was able to see the Lord, high and lifted up; His train filling the temple (Isaiah 6:1)! In the New Covenant we learn that the temple of God is His people (1 Corinthians 3:16-17). Us! Once the bearer of the Adamic trademark who lifted his heart up against God was dead, spiritual eyes came open. One would really appreciate the impact of the spiritual breakthrough upon reading the Book of Isaiah which is filled with prophetic richness concerning our Lord. As long as the false entity is in view, people will never see the true.

This is a great time to acknowledge those with hearts to do the will of God His Way. The priests who tried to prevent the trespass of Uzziah are well noted. They are likened to those today who realize racial prejudice is wrong and intervene on behalf of what is right. God will always have a remnant unto Himself. May God bless each bondservant bountifully. Imagine no salt or light in this present evil world.

Such an account as king Uzziah's is noted that we may see the far-reaching effect of the disobedience unleashed by Adam. Would it not be more blessed to live in a kingdom of prosperity and great security with God's oversight that in one under the judgment of a disobedient leader? Uzziah remained a leper all his days cut off from the house of the Lord.

Deuteronomy, Chapter 8, contains a warning to the children of Israel to keep God's commands so as not to forget Him and lift their hearts against Him. Pride is a simple way of saying the heart is lifted up. For God knew that once a people became prosperous, they were likely to forget Him and His ways and do as they were pleased. His commands are not grievous but rather for man's well-being. The fallen nature will never embrace this fact.

Love is patient, love is kind. It does not envy, it does not boast, it is not proud.

1 Corinthians 13:4

CHAPTER 3

A MASTER OF DISGUISE

Do NOT BE FOOLED AT THE SPIRIT BEHIND THE FALLEN NATURE. IT IS astounding how so many including believers underestimate Satan's ability to transform himself into an angel or messenger of light (2 Corinthians 11:14). This means there are no holds barred when he attempts to imitate the heavenly glory. When the Apostle Paul was warning the Corinthians, he was afraid that like the serpent beguiled Eve their minds would be corrupted from the simplicity that is in Christ. The warning was of receiving another Gospel, another Jesus, and another spirit if they rejected the truth. He also warned of false apostles and deceitful workers transforming themselves into the apostles of Christ. Satan's ability is the ability given to the false prophet. Awake and arise!

An accuser must always find convincing ways to support his false claims. The great seducer is not often challenged for this very reason. His tactics are so convincing and bewitching. He masterfully makes it all seem to be in the best interest of the ones being seduced, usually to make them appear better than all the others. Consequently, those not Spirit-filled follow such a one in droves right into a snare.

Such deceivers are powered by a spiritual force emanating from a defeated foe and his kingdom. This foe works through the fallen nature. That means it must be given power. Without being given such power, such a one would have no platform from which to exploit others. For instance, if there is a summon to gather to perpetuate hate and no one shows up, hate receives no power or influence whatsoever? None!

Many years ago, during a season of preparation, God gave me several dreams and visions. Some are indelibly etched into my memory and for good reason. They are spiritual dreams and visions that include both God's warning and guidance. They are relevant to this very day and always will be.

In the early years of ministry, I dreamed about a large white background. A pure bright white background comparable to a super huge canvas. In the middle of the background from top to bottom was a large serpent which blended in perfectly until he moved. I repeat, this was a solid bright white background. Every time the serpent made the slightest move, I could see the outline of his scales shift. When he stopped moving, he blended back into the background as though not there at all. Although he tried to move without my notice, I saw every move he made. This went on for a while until I finally looked at the bottom corner of the background and that is when his cover was fully blown because he had two slivers of red eyes that were impossible to conceal. He could not conceal his means of enchantment! Thank You, Jesus!

The dream reminded me of leviathan described in Job Chapter 41. God revealed to me the great length the enemy goes to deceive us, but the greater revelation is that he cannot hide at all if seen through the eyes of the Spirit. He is a most formidable foe until seen through Redemption. I have gained so much from this one dream but important in this discussion is a note from Job 41:15 which reads, "His scales are his pride, shut up together as with a close seal."

This enemy feels so shielded in his self confidence that he believes he is invincible. Feed his pride with fear and help create a monster! Not so through our God! Matthew 24:24 admonishes us to be watchful because there shall arise false Christs, and false prophets, and shall shew great signs and wonders insomuch that, if it were possible, they shall deceive the very elect. Praise God who makes it impossible for His elect to be deceived.

But put ye on the Lord Jesus Christ, and make not provision for the flesh, to fulfil the lusts thereof.

Romans 13:14

CHAPTER 4

HEAVENLY ATTRIBUTES LOST

IN VERSES 3-5 OF EZEKIEL CHAPTER 28, GOD ACKNOWLEDGES THE attributes with which He graced the man. The man's wisdom is compared to that of Daniel which any believer recognizes as out of the ordinary with the ability to save others from harm. God allowed Daniel to see secret or hidden things and that wisdom is sorely lacking in the Church and lives of believers today.

Calamity would not be overtaking mankind in the way it is if leaders' hearts were pure before God. Those of us who live in the Spirit are not surprised by any of the current events and are well prepared for them naturally and spiritually. There are those who know the signs of the times and what God's people ought to be doing.

In these verses God pointed out how the man used his great wisdom and understanding to get riches of gold and silver into his treasures. His wisdom along with his trafficking increased his riches. Together, these represent the root cause of his heart being lifted up against God. Mixture abounds in these verses, but it is such a common thing in regular "ministry" today until one may easily miss the problem being revealed. Trafficking or merchandizing has been given the same place in many churches as in the world system.

The wisdom of God is found in Christ Jesus. 1 Corinthians 1:30 declares that He has been made unto us wisdom. Gold and silver are precious metals which carry powerful spiritual significance. Gold refers to our divine nature in God and silver speaks to redemption. Their significance is being traded off or trafficked in ignorance. They are treasures belonging to God that are not for a man's personal treasury. God's people are a peculiar treasure to Him.

The man used his wisdom to traffic and bring in more riches. Today, it looks like all the merchandizing one sees going on in the church. Same as back in the day when Jesus cleansed the temple. At that time, the very things that were to be used for offerings unto God were being sold at exorbitant prices. Same Adamic trademark! As then even now we need the Master of the house to cleanse it.

Because of the lucrative side of many ministries, some totally separate from God. The telltale sign is when one stops preaching the Gospel and belabors the people with personal kingdom-building undertakings under the guise of ministry from God. Throwing His holy Name around once in a great while is not making Him the center where His rightful place is. Once things get so big and influential in such a carnal machine, politicians often come calling and the sellout intensifies. Just repent and do it God's way. Walk after the spirit and not after the flesh and when that happens, God said there is no condemnation to those in Christ Jesus (Romans 8:1).

Quickly referring back to Daniel, remember how he survived the lion's den? Although the angels (messengers) shut the mouths of the lions, a deeper revelation is there. When heavenly messengers or Godly ministers speak forth truth, it shuts the mouths of our enemies. 1 Peter 5:8 declares, "Be sober, be vigilant; because your adversary the devil, as a roaring lion, walketh about, seeking whom he may devour." God was so pleased with Daniel's obedience until those lions could see no flesh at all. Oops! Nothing to eat!

Keep in mind we are tracking the decline of the man once separated from God. The decline has only begun now that his heart is set as the heart of God and judgement is declared. May we lay our personal ideas of judgment aside and instead lay the Cross of Christ over it. In righteousness He judges and makes war (Revelation 19:11).

Carnality cannot change carnality. If only everyone knew and embraced that point. Respond in the flesh and flesh will result. If we truly desire enduring change, we will see this whole thing God's way from now on. We are in a time where a re-set is a requirement not a choice if one is not already living in the Spirit.

So God created man in his own image, in the image of God created he him; male and female created he them.

Genesis 1:27

CHAPTER 5

RIGHTEOUS JUDGMENT

THE VERSES OF EZEKIEL 28:6-10 ARE SO CHOCKED FULL OF WISDOM and power to the hearing ear and receiving heart. There is instant empowerment by God. First, because the man set his heart as the heart of God, "strangers" would be brought upon him. Who are they and what can these strangers do to one with the Adamic residue?

As believers we are pilgrims and strangers in this world. First Peter 2:11 practically begs us like so, "Dearly beloved, I beseech you as strangers and pilgrims, abstain from fleshly lusts, which war against the soul." We are in this world but not of it and employ differing weapons of warfare that are not carnal but mighty through God to the pulling down of strongholds (2 Corinthians 10:4).

No matter how "justified" or cathartic a revengeful reaction may feel, racial prejudice will not be eliminated through carnal warfare. When the phantom Adam is pushed back, he simply regroups. People blame wrong things on a devil, but it is actually the unregenerate man, the devil's agent, doing his thing. Never forget that wickedness is his energy supply. Racism is only a byproduct which is why we must see the situation spiritually.

The Life of Christ Jesus must be ministered through us. Not the "by-and-by Jesus" that emerged from the fallen man's psyche, but the Lord from heaven Who came along with our Heavenly Father to live within His Body as He promised. Retaliation must be through love, peace, and His power. Vengeance belongs to God.

As strangers from heavenly Jerusalem we are the "terrible of the nations" who draw out our swords (the Word of God) against the beauty of the wisdom of this fallen man and take him down. In the words of the late John Lewis, we need to understand the true spirit of "good trouble." Good trouble is standing for what is right without trespassing God's command to love one another!

With the Word of God or Christ flowing within us, we defile Adam's fake "brightness." It is not the true light. One will not be able to comprehend what the false is until the true Light appears. Remember, Simon the sorcerer was considered the great power of God until the true apostles showed up in God's Power and blew his cover and shut him down (Acts 8). His fake "brightness" was revealed as nothing but darkness and was rebuked the moment the Light of Christ shined through the apostles. Simon's bewitching powers were no match and although he believed, he still wanted to try to buy the Power of God. Impossible! This "brightness" will be zoomed later.

God further decreed that this man would be brought down to the pit to die the deaths of them that are slain in the midst of the seas. This is precisely what happened to Adam in the Cross. As one can see with an open heart, many died with Adam "in the midst of the seas" (Ezekiel 28: 8 reads, "They shall bring thee down to the pit, and thou shalt die the deaths of them that are slain in the midst of the seas)."

Isaiah 57:20 helps us better understand the reference to the "seas". It reads, "But the wicked are like the troubled sea, when it cannot rest, whose waters cast up mire and dirt." Iniquity or wickedness was found in Adam and therein lies the great breach that started it all. This Federal head of iniquity affected all mankind.

The nature of the old man would have no "life" if people would turn to God. Ever heard of dying to self? When people demonstrate the behavior of the "prince of Tyrus" or Adam, they are ignorant of what is true of them from the heavenly perspective and are merely the true walking dead! Jesus did away with the old man as the following Scripture chart clearly shows. Carefully weigh each step and ask the Holy Spirit to lead us through each step experientially.

THIS IS WHAT HAPPENED TO OUR OLD NATURE IN ADAM!

1. CRUCIFIED WITH CHRIST

Romans 6:6 Knowing this, that <u>our old man is crucified with [him]</u>, that the body of sin might be destroyed, that henceforth we should not serve sin.

Galatians 2:20 <u>I am crucified with Christ</u>: nevertheless I live; yet not I, but Christ lives in me: and the life which I now live in the flesh I live by the faith of the Son of God, who loved me, and gave himself for me.

Galatians 6:14 But God forbid that I should glory, save in the cross of our Lord Jesus Christ, by whom <u>the world is crucified unto me, and I unto the world.</u>

2. DIED WITH CHRIST

Romans 6:8 Now if we be <u>dead with Christ</u>, we believe that we shall also live with him:

Colossians 3:3 For ye are dead, and your life is hid with Christ in God.

3. BURIED WITH CHRIST

Romans 6:4 Therefore we are <u>buried with him</u> by baptism into death: that like as Christ was raised up from the dead by the glory of the Father, even so we also should walk in newness of life.

Note: Please do not bring the fallen man (OLD NATURE) up because a new creation was quickened, raised and seated in Christ.

Continuing in Ezekiel 28:9-10 (KJV), we begin to close in on the spirit of this nature. God said, "Wilt thou yet say before him that slayeth thee, I am God? But thou shalt be a man, and no God, in the hand of him that slayeth thee. Thou shalt die the deaths of the uncircumcised by the hand of strangers: for I have spoken it, saith the Lord God."

At the unveiling of Christ in one, Adam's power becomes fully diminished! (Notice the phrase is "unveiling *in* one" versus "unveiling *to* one"). The only One Who can slay Adam for us experientially is Christ Jesus within. Man is just a man and not God. When the Power of God slayed Adam through the obedience of Christ Jesus on the Cross, he was powerless to withstand Him. Jesus took on the force of sin drawing it into Himself, and it was crucified with Him. Read the chart above again to seal the truth of what happened to the old man in our minds and hearts. We must understand that a new creature came forth in the Resurrection.

"To die the deaths of the uncircumcised" illuminates the lack of a covenant between God and the man. Circumcision in that time meant an act had taken place to ratify a covenant between God and man. Praise God for in the New Covenant through the Blood of Jesus Christ we now have a Mediator of righteousness living within! See why we must preach the Gospel! May we put our programs and projects aside and preach Christ and Him crucified and what that means to us all! No longer give place to the fallen nature which only looks out for itself. People are experiencing enough destruction and death, and the time is now for His Life and that more abundantly.

And I, if I be lifted up from the earth,
will draw all men unto me.

John 12:32

CHAPTER 6

EDEN'S EDICT IGNORED

EZEKIEL 28: 12-15, DRAWS OUT THE SPIRITUAL FORCE BEHIND THE REAL problem of racial prejudice to the forefront. Bottom line up front, the fallen nature is attempting to recoup a former glory, and the natural man will never be able to restore the magnificence and beauty he had in Eden. That man was covered with the glory of the Light of God. Out of fallen man's emptiness, he uses skin color as a means of self "glorification". At times he foolishly includes "righteousness" as something relating to his fallen nature under the cloak of his skin.

Often, the lighter the skin, the more special or accepted one is deemed. This stems from a longing for the former glory. Character, resourcefulness, creativity, and myriads of other powerful attributes are shielded behind hatred or instantly assassinated in an ignorant perception based on skin color. It is amazing how few are interested in understanding the origin of this attitude. Think about it for a moment. How many people have ever stopped to consider why so many are obsessed with the color of one's skin? Why? Let us continue digging until the root is completely exposed so it may wither, dry up and die giving way to a beautiful, multicolored humanity of love and harmony from which Christ glows.

God reiterated the original man's beauty in Ezekiel, Chapter 28:17 (KJV). "Son of man, take up a lamentation upon the king of Tyrus, and say unto him, Thus saith the Lord God; Thou sealest up the sum, full of wisdom, and perfect in beauty." This was a representative man for all mankind called Adam. He was full of God's Substance and perfect in beauty! "Thou hast been in Eden the garden of God (Ezekiel 28:13)." In Eden, the man along with his wife received an edict. If we are to get to the root of it all we must patiently and thoroughly examine it.

"And the LORD God planted a garden eastward in Eden; and there he put the man whom he had formed." Gen. 2:8, KJV

Our loving Creator planted a garden eastward in Eden where He placed the man He had formed. The root meaning of *garden* is manifold including to *defend, cover, surround or hedge about*. The first man's habitation was a place of protection, plenty, and peace as well as a full expression of God's Substance within him and surrounding him. The garden was situated eastward in *Eden* which means *pleasure*. Eden is derived from a meaning so intensely rich that it takes such words as luxury, dainty, delight, finery to help one grasp its essence. What a glorious state of existence and environment of unimpeded relationship between God and man!

The garden in the fullness of its meaning encapsulates unfathomable truths. Song of Solomon sheds light on God's intent for it and the man He put there. Song 4:12, 16 reads, "A garden enclosed *is* my sister, *my* spouse; a spring shut up, a fountain sealed. Awake, O north wind; and come, thou south; blow upon my garden, *that* the spices thereof may flow out. Let my beloved come into his garden and eat his pleasant fruits." An omniscient God knew the Fall would occur and the garden, though a place, ultimately spoke to Christ and His Church.

Gen. 2:9 "And out of the ground made the LORD God to grow every tree that is pleasant to the sight, and good for food; the tree of life also in the midst of the garden, and the tree of knowledge of good and evil."

Notice that the trees were *pleasant to the sight* and *good for food.* The Word of God contains an incalculable amount of revelation for the hearing ear. It is critical to note the order of emphasis God placed on the purpose of the trees. First, they were *"pleasant to the sight."* Above, it is noted that Eden already means pleasure; however, God saw fit to magnify the pleasure that the trees could afford one's sight.

Let us shift from the trees for a moment and focus on what God means by *sight.* The Hebrew meaning for the word translated *sight* is *appearance or vision.* Vision in this sense relates to the supernatural. It also means *to see, look at, inspect, perceive, consider.* The words perceive and consider both take on a more significant meaning than simply beholding a thing with the natural eye. They connote insight. To every overcomer, it should be apparent that we are now on higher ground in thought.

Next, it is written that the trees were *"good for food."* Everything God made He had already declared "good" yet again we find Divine emphasis where the trees are concerned. The word good used here allies itself with words such as *pleasant* and *agreeable* in capturing God's thought in His description of the trees. The food provided by the trees was not only pleasing to the appetite, but apparently had a satisfying quality within it that was all sufficient making it most agreeable to the man.

There were two specific trees that were distinct from the others. In the midst of the garden was the tree of life and the tree of the knowledge of good and evil. For the moment let us focus on the latter. God gave concise instructions to the man regarding the tree of the knowledge of good and evil. "And the LORD God took the man and put him into the garden of Eden to dress it and to keep it. And the LORD God commanded the man, saying, Of every tree of the garden thou mayest freely eat: But of the tree of the knowledge of good and evil, thou shalt not eat of it: for in the day that thou eat thereof thou shalt surely die." True then, true now.

God gave the man a woman. The woman, Eve, was beguiled by the serpent and ate of the forbidden tree of the knowledge of good and evil. She gave of the fruit thereof to Adam, her husband. Together, they speak to the spirit (inner man) and soul (mind, will, and emotions). Adam represents the spirit and Eve represents the soul.

As noted previously, the Apostle Paul embraced this analogy when he warned the Church at Corinth of the spiritual significance of Eve's act of disobedience. He told them, "But I fear, lest by any means, as the serpent beguiled Eve through his subtilty, so your minds should be corrupted from the simplicity that is in Christ (2 Corinthians 11:3)." Notice the Apostle Paul linked "minds" directly to Eve. The deceiver targets and can only get a foothold through the mind. Let us revisit the deception.

"Now the serpent was more subtle than any beast of the field which the LORD God had made. And he said unto the woman, Yea, hath God said, Ye shall not eat of every tree of the garden? And the woman said unto the serpent, We may eat of the fruit of the trees of the garden: But of the fruit of the tree which is in the midst of the garden, God hath said, Ye shall not eat of it, neither shall ye touch it, lest ye die. And the serpent said unto the woman, Ye shall not surely die: For God doth know that in the day ye eat thereof, then your eyes shall be opened, and ye shall be as gods, knowing good and evil. And when the woman saw that the tree was good for food, and that it was pleasant to the eyes, and a tree to be desired to make one wise, she took of the fruit thereof, and did eat, and gave also unto her husband with her; and he did eat. And the eyes of them both were opened, and they knew that they were naked; and they sewed fig leaves together and made themselves aprons (Genesis 3:1-7 KJV)."

Subtle is a perfect word to describe the serpent. When one is hedged in a garden surrounded by and filled with all that is pleasant and good, a cunning persuasion by that which hates God and his perfect creation slithers in through the only penetrable entry, the mind. Sadly, it happens too readily in the lives of many. Our position in Christ means we are back in our Heavenly Father's presence and favor, and despite the pleasantness and spiritual power, deceit vies with truth in minds and hearts. Too often the deceit is engaged instead of being cast out.

God had a Divine Order or Precedence in the way man, who is spirit first, was to acknowledge and use the trees He planted. This writer refers to it as Eden's Edict. First, God said the trees were "…pleasant to the sight and secondly, good for food…" After the cunning serpent beguiled Eve, she "saw" something very differently and changed God's Order in her heart because of her now distorted, erroneous, lowly, carnal, view. "And when the woman saw that the tree *was* good for food, and that it *was* pleasant to the eyes, and a tree to be desired to make *one* wise, she took of the fruit thereof, and did eat, and gave also unto her husband with her; and he did eat." It may have even been hard for the reader to note what is now different. Subtlety hides easily yet its ability is not diminished.

The trees that were once foremost *pleasant to the sight* and spoke to their ability to perceive spiritually and accurately were now ineffective. All things had become carnal! Now, the new order for them was first "*good for food.*" In other words, things had to appeal to the flesh first and spiritual things were no longer relevant. Praise God for Jesus being Spirit-led when the tempter came trying to capitalize on His hunger after fasting forty days. Knowing the difference between that which is spiritual and that which is carnal or that which is temporal and that which is eternal, He overcame. Spirit first!

Secondly, Eve "saw" the tree of the knowledge of good and evil was *"pleasant to the eyes."* Did you note how the deception actually changed the Word of God in her being? Again, God said, *"pleasant to the sight,"* and it was first in His Order. Now, she heard, *pleasant to the eyes.* The words *"sight"* and *"eyes"* carry two different meanings in this context and two different words are used to teach us. *Eyes* speak to natural sight in this passage. Be most particular to note that all spiritual things have now departed.

Further, note that after her deception she "saw" something that God did not mention in Genesis 2:9. Now added was *"...a tree to be desired to make one wise."* The true intent of God for a thing was now shrouded in carnality. Now suddenly there is a "desire" that was unknown previously. In spirit all sufficiency is of God; therefore, a desire for something other than God apparently arose from another source. Again, referring to the Apostle Paul's address to the Corinthians, his fear was they would hear "another gospel" and receive "another Jesus" not preached to them.

The deception placed an unnecessary burden on the man and woman. Consequently, they had to attempt to figure things out instead of walking with God in the "cool" or *spirit* of the day and operating in full spiritual discernment. No longer spiritually cognizant of God's purpose for the trees, Adam and Eve used the leaves of a fig tree to cover their nakedness. They hid from God as if that is truly possible. God loves His creation so much that encrypted in Adam's response to God's call to him is a powerful truth. God is love. Adam responded, "I heard thy voice in the garden, and I was afraid, because I *was* naked; and I hid myself." The Hebrew word for "hid" is the same as "love" as found in Deuteronomy 33: 3," Yea, he loved the people."

Every believer must know that God's love has not changed, and He has restored mankind through the obedience of the last Adam, Jesus Christ our Lord. Nothing can separate us from the love of Christ! Romans 8: 35, 37-39 assures: Who shall separate us from the love of Christ? shall tribulation, or distress, or persecution, or famine, or nakedness, or peril, or sword? Nay, in all these things we are more than conquerors through him that loved us. For I am persuaded, that neither death, nor life, nor angels, nor principalities, nor powers, nor things present, nor things to come, Nor height, nor depth, nor any other creature, shall be able to separate us from the love of God, which is in Christ Jesus our Lord.

Genesis 3:24 reads,

"So he drove out the man; and he placed at the east of the garden of Eden Cherubims, and a flaming sword which turned every way, to keep the way of the tree of life." There is a common but false perception that because the man was driven out, the garden no longer exists. We just read that the way of the tree of life is being kept by a flaming sword. Spiritually speaking, the Spirit of the fulfilled Word of God is keeping the way of the tree of life.

Often the letter which kills is "ministered;" however, when the Spirit of the Word is ministered in power, it becomes evident that Eden speaks to our position in Christ. Second Corinthians 3:6 tells us that God, "hath made us able ministers of the new testament; not of the letter, but of the spirit: for the letter kills, but the spirit giveth life." This same able ministry is described by the Prophet Joel in Chapter 2:3 when he saw, "A fire devours before them; and behind them a flame burns: the land is as the garden of Eden before them, and behind them a desolate wilderness; yea, and nothing shall escape them." Our God is a consuming fire. He goes before us and is our Rear Guard. Christ Jesus is the Way of the Spirit in which we travel and as we pass through in Him in our ascent, nothing is behind that we ever wish to return to. Eden and all that it represents remains in its pristine fullness in Christ.

The serpent's method of operating never changes. Be ever mindful of this fact. Whether he presents as the serpent, devil, adversary, accuser, or simply and most often, the carnal mind, he will always employ the same method of appealing to the lust of the flesh, the lust of the eyes and the pride of life. First John 2:16 reads, "For all that is in the world, the lust of the flesh, and the lust of the eyes, and the pride of life, is not of the Father, but is of the world."

As seen earlier, The Apostle Paul warned the Corinthians and with love, these words carry the same message. Through Christ, refuse to allow the deception of the carnal mind to corrupt the simplicity that is found only in Him. Remember, "But every man is tempted, when he is drawn away of his own lust, and enticed. Then when lust has conceived, it brings forth sin: and sin, when it is finished, brings forth death" (James 1:14-15).

May we all stop blaming a devil whose works were destroyed when the Son of God was manifested (I John 3:8) and rather put on the Lord Jesus Christ, and make no provision for the flesh, to fulfil the lusts thereof (Romans 13:14). We are told to walk or live in the Spirit, so as not to fulfil the lust of the flesh (Galatians 5:16).

Whoever claims to love God yet hates a brother or sister is a liar. For whoever does not love their brother and sister, whom they have seen, cannot love God, whom they have not seen.

1 John 4:20, NIV

And he has given us this command: Anyone who loves God must also love their brother and sister.

1 John 4:21, NIV

CHAPTER 7

THE TAPROOT:
THE LOSS OF HIS BRIGHTNESS

"EVERY PRECIOUS STONE WAS THY COVERING, THE SARDIUS, TOPAZ, AND the diamond, the beryl, the onyx, and the jasper, the sapphire, the emerald, and the carbuncle, and gold: the workmanship of thy tabrets and of thy pipes was prepared in thee in the day that thou was created." Ten stones of perfect beauty were traded for death which would lead to Law or that by which man would know what sin is. (One meaning for the number 10 in the Bible is Law).

We have found the taproot! Here we have the heart of the force behind racial and all other prejudices! The man's covering of Light or his brightness was lost so he devised his own version of glory in his darkened heart. The closer he appears in his own mind to naturally resemble that from which he fell fills him with conceit. Mind you it is fallen man's perception of light and not God's. White or light skin is not the covering of the Light of God.

In the Fall, the exchange was spiritual not natural. Multiplied millions of people are ostracized, criticized, traumatized, and demonized simply for the color of their skin. Let us not ignore that white people experience racial prejudice also but more than less the target is generally people of color. We must maintain honesty and transparency in this treatise.

To all God's innocent children reading this book who are white, there is no intention whatsoever to hurt or to take a swipe at you but rather to make a critical point. For many, your brotherly kindness, love and goodness have helped many, and you are continuing to do so. Many of you are as baffled at racial prejudice as people of color are. You are an example of the love of our Savior, Jesus Christ and reflect His glory. On the other hand, there are those who epitomize evil with raw and vicious hatred for no reason whatsoever except to appear to be better in their own eyes than those unlike themselves

If we are going to be truthful, we cannot keep hiding our heads in the sand as though nothing is wrong. The only one truly at fault for this evil is a disobedient man, Adam, and Jesus Christ has dealt with him thereby destroying the works of the devil (1 John 3:8). We all must now learn what Jesus did in His dealings with the fallen man and who we all are now in Christ. There is a life that is higher!

Again, for emphasis, that which is at the center of racial prejudice is the color of the skin. By and large great lengths are often taken to separate those who are white from all others. A person born to a white parent and a nonwhite parent is automatically identified with the nonwhite parent. Why? These are actual situations that people ignore, and it is time to take these things out of the dusty storage box of evil that keeps showing up on the far corner shelves of the hearts of mankind.

Do not think for once that all the blame of racism is being shifted onto white people. No race is exempt. Racism is derived from a spiritual evil that will work in anyone willing to allow it. Also, there are many prejudices within groups where one will find differences made based on the color on one's skin. No matter who prejudice works through, it is simply a futile attempt at self-glorification.

Remaining honest and transparent, White people have dominated and enjoyed privilege whether earned or not while others have been marginalized in many disparaging ways. Many have been misled into believing that God set it up this way. A separatist label has emerged called privilege that for many has become an unspoken right with total disregard for the rights of others.

Remember, the blame is not with anyone in particular, but a spiritual influence of unbridled fear and ignorance of what the Redemptive Work of Jesus Christ truly exacted. What we see today is an entity who has bewitched a people and formed a kingdom of those who rightfully belong to Kingdom of God. Blame is but a spark of a universal wildfire. Wake up!

Either we get it right now or we will keep going around the mountain generation after generation spiraling while helplessly tossed back and forth in a dust devil of evil. Literally, because the man formed from the dust of the ground is not in charge! This is not about trying to change minds but hearts instead. Our minds must be transformed and only God can do that. Every other attempt at it is temporal and just lulls the monster to sleep for brief while.

The way to effectively get over being "sick and tired" of it all is to give Christ His rightful place. The truth is we all are victims here because of one man's disobedience. Adam! This attempt to regain his "brightness" brings out his fallen nature of fear, death and destruction that work in tandem within people because of separation from God.

Look at history! Choose any period you like. It is full of destruction: wars, greed, feverish acquisition of the most and best, towers to heaven, disregard for the poor, callous, calculating, and an unbridled lascivious heart. By the way, what was just described transcends race. We have been given a more excellent ministry that raises us all above this present evil by Christ Jesus, and we must walk in it.

Ezekiel 28 continues, "…the workmanship of thy tabrets and of thy pipes was prepared in thee in the day that thou was created." His praise and his glory were prepared in him when he was created. Tabrets are what we call tambourines today. They are instruments of praise. The word "pipes" needs deeper clarification. Many believe all this has to do with a devil who used to lead the choir in heaven but was kicked out. Please!

We have already learned that this is a "man" who was in Eden. That is Adam! "Pipes" are the same as a bezel or groove that holds a gem in place in a piece of jewelry. Notice his pipes were created in him not something he adds to himself. Skin color and heavenly glory are not the same.

Because we are created to worship God in spirit and in truth, the fallen man set up his own idea of what glory is supposed to look like. Nothing new! Remember he thought fig leaves would help them blend in with the garden as though God could not see them. Whatever man covers himself with is always hiding something else! He outwardly tries to hide his inward heart.

We need to land here for a brief moment because much of this faux "glory" has filtered into and is dominating in the Church. Enough already! For example, vestments do not equate to power and purity nor distinction over others. We are called to be servants one to another. On the other hand, designer clothing and accessories afford the same empty spiritual weight as vestments. This is not to condemn and of course do what you like while cognizant that nothing outward is important here. What can one possibly put on that carries a greater weight of glory than the Anointed One?

Back to the central theme, there is as much racial prejudice, along with its fake glory, in some churches as it is in the world system. Mind you we are talking about only one form of prejudice. There are many other forms, but the emphasis is on race because we are all God's children, and it is critically essential that we deal with it right now! Once the root problem of a fallen man attempting to usurp the glory of the Promised Son is exposed, understood, and embraced, we can all begin to heal. Then and only then can the other important areas such as gender, age and other prejudices receive the same attention simultaneously and be healed also. The way of the Lord is 100% better.

One cannot conjure up the glory of God. We are meant to go from glory to glory. That has nothing to do with shades of skin. It is written, "But we all, with open face beholding as in a glass the glory of the Lord, are changed into the same image from glory to glory, [even] as by the Spirit of the Lord (2 Corinthians 3:18." As the Spirit of God works in us, we become more and more like Christ reflecting His glory like mirrors. Just as Stephen's face shone like an angel (Acts 6:15), so shall the world see Christ in His people.

Jesus said, "Ye are the light of the world. A city that is set on a hill cannot be hid (Matthew 5:14)." He also said, "... I am the light of the world: he that followeth me shall not walk in darkness, but shall have the light of life (John 8:12)." Jesus was the Word made Flesh and John called Him the true Light, which lights every man that cometh into the world (John 1:9). Again, man cannot force this glory.

An early technological feat of Texas Instruments was that they developed what is called Digital Light Processing or DLP. DLP is a digital micro mirror device chip that is covered with thousands of aluminum mirrors. Light shining on the chip directs individual light beams through a lens for a clear and enhanced image. This technology is a great representation of who we are in Christ. Many "chips" reflecting the True Light! Many members yet one Body called Christ (1 Corinthians 12:12).

The only race that is a factor here is the Spirit Race in Christ. And as we have borne the image of the earthy, we shall also bear the image of the heavenly (I Corinthians 15:49): therefore, let your light so shine before men, that they may see your good works, and glorify your Father which is in heaven (Matthew 5:16)."

God's glory is His and to get back to this pristine state in Him one must believe and put on the Lord Jesus Christ. He is our armor of Light. The Church must minister the real Christ and not a man's version of Him! The true "pipe" or bezel in the new creation man is the open heart fully turned to God our Father which He will fill with his love and wisdom. It is that aspect of Christ that we embrace and exemplify through obedience. His brightness! That is how this evil of racism can begin its descent into the abyss of the "midst of the seas."

The Adamic nature is a dangerous and a deadly phantom of an outlaw spirit. Through Christ may we change racism to "gracism." Despite all the recent ministering on the subject of grace from every nook and cranny of Churchdom, many remain content to proceed broken as though nothing is wrong. Ministers still pounce from thrones on pulpits to illuminate the problem but never invoke the inexhaustible sufficiency of God's grace.

Grace is not a transitional theme making its round on the circuit. Grace is that which along with truth came by Jesus Christ and through faith in Him mankind receives salvation. If we would preach Christ, we would see grace as a perpetual theme alongside love and truth. Condensed version is the Gospel of Jesus Christ! The wizard of this world has seduced many into complacency or many just choose to look the other way. Praise God for those who see it all for what it is. Wake up slumbering saints! Do you really think the way things are presently is God's will for us all?

Many churches are knee deep in league with the world system. Some religious leaders kowtow to politicians for filthy lucre and sell out themselves and their people. This is all the residue of Babylon's mixture. Let us take a moment to see the outcome of it all which The Book of the Revelation of Jesus Christ calls the Great Whore. She is none other than Mystery Babylon with her web of confusion.

When people wake up to spiritual things in Christ, there will be weeping and gnashing of teeth for real. When many see how they have been duped into becoming instruments of evil through things such a racism, they will be greatly ashamed. Just a puppet of a fallen system. Wealthy, powerful, influential but still just a puppet. If you are a racist, no matter what race or color your skin is, you are being used and you are a mere commodity in Babylon. Mind you dear reader, that system falls only at the unveiling, uncovering, or revelation of Jesus Christ. No man's race, creed or national origin will help him here.

For a snapshot of Mystery Babylon's demise let us look at this brazen whore who calls herself a "queen." She is an affront to God and gives the fallen man such a well-grounded foothold in the lives of people.

"...I sit a queen, and am no widow, and shall see no sorrow."
Revelation 18:7

In the Revelation of Jesus Christ, Mystery Babylon is uncovered and destroyed. This is a fact and not a future event for those who live in the Spirit. Again, for emphasis, notice intently that she is thoroughly exposed only as Jesus Christ is unveiled. All the things the enemy twisted to scare believers away from the Truth of our Lord in the Book of Revelation, actually point us to His eternal Work of Redemption. Once He is seen, all that is not like Him is seen for the great illusion it all is. Compared to Christ even the best of that which opposes Him is nothing. In reading the Book of Revelation, the Bride of the Lamb is seen only after Mystery Babylon, the Counterfeit Queen, is destroyed. Hear it well!

Several things are certain of Mystery Babylon from Revelation, Chapter 17 where she is judged. She is the one with whom the kings of the earth committed fornication, and the inhabitants of the earth were made drunk with her fornication. Idolatry! Idolatry! Idolatry! Racism creates an idol. She arrays herself in royal colors of purple and scarlet and decks herself with gold and precious stones and pearls. How she looks the part! This is the reason why she seduces many so easily. The one who claims to be a queen is none other than that great harlot city which is a lustful magnet for the kings of the earth. Be careful to note the fraud she perpetrates because The Revelation also describes the true City of God, the Bride of Christ, and in comparison, Mystery Babylon's counterfeit is glaring!

Babylon the great is fallen, is fallen! This is true presently for those living in the Spirit. Therefore, evils such as racism can be eradicated if people want them to be. This self-proclaimed queen is not only fallen but is the habitation of devils, the hold every foul spirit, and the cage of every unclean and hateful bird (Revelation 18:2). A habitation, a hold, and a cage but not a queen! Upon close scrutiny of her acts, one finds that not only are all the nations drunk of the wine of the wrath of her fornication, and the kings of the earth have committed fornication with her, but also the merchants of the earth made their fortunes through the abundance of her "luxuries."

John heard a voice commanding God's people to come out of her so they would not be partakers of her sins and receive not of her plagues. This self-appointed queen has glorified herself and lived luxuriously at the expense of the people. By Christ Jesus, her double reward is exacted. In one day, her plagues came. That day was the day Jesus Christ of

Nazareth was crucified, carrying the sin of the world with Him. By His obedience unto death, her judgment came in one day. Death, mourning, and famine at once as she is snuffed out by the Fire of God.

"Those that fared sumptuously with her shall weep and wail for her (Revelation 18:15)." It looks like this: The capitalists of the world and the charlatans in the Church that used her to dominate and exploit God's people no longer have a cloak of darkness to move under and are utterly exposed. As people receive a revelation of what the Lord Jesus Christ has done for and as them in His Redemptive Work, every trace of this counterfeit will be blasted from their hearts and minds. Her residue is replaced as people put on the mind of Christ. She has nothing to feed on in regenerated saints and is utterly tormented. The Day of the Lord is here! Kings see her torment and burning. According to Revelation 1:6, Jesus has made us kings and priests unto God through His shed Blood. As we stand in our rightful position in the Spirit, we can see her demise clearly. No one buys the merchandize of fear and exploitation she afforded the merchants. Her might has disintegrated in Christ!

The Revelation, Chapter 18 names the merchandize. Verses 12-13 lists them as the merchandise of gold, and silver, and precious stones, and of pearls, and fine linen, and purple, and silk, and scarlet, and all thyine wood, and all manner vessels of ivory, and all manner vessels of most precious wood, and of brass, and iron, and marble, and cinnamon, and odors, and ointments, and frankincense, and wine, and oil, and fine flour, and wheat, and beasts, and sheep, and horses, and chariots, and slaves, and souls of men. And! And! And! Finally, the spiritual issue, the "souls of men" lands at the end for emphasis!

Hopefully, the reader has noticed the souls of men are a mere commodity in the harlot church system. Just "stuff" to be traded. Insignificant except for "goods" to be trafficked! Yes, souls of men! Face it! One probably believes he or she is very important in his or her "ministry" and the world just cannot do without them. Look at it all again through Spiritual lenses! The will of God is all that matters here! God's children are not to be bought or sold. There should be no "carrots" dangling in the Church. No one should have to sell out or compromise for a temporal position.

We are all members in particular in the Body of Christ. Because of the Cross and Its appropriation, the lusts of the souls vanish and shall not be found again in the counterfeit. The mind, will, and emotions which make up the soul were manipulated beyond measure in Mystery Babylon making it impossible to yield to the inner man of the heart. In Christ, the souls of men are under the control of the renewed spirit in Him.

As the merchants mourn her, they reminisce about her outward show which they perceived as her glory. They remembered that she was clothed in fine linen, purple, and scarlet, and decked with gold, and precious stones, and pearls! Here is why outward appearance means nothing. The Bible says that the fine linen is the righteousness of saints (Revelation 19:8). Oh, how she has fooled multitudes!

Her outward pomp of wearing heavenly, royal colors of purple and scarlet would fool the elect if it were possible. She gave the illusion that she was noble (purple) and Blood-bought (scarlet). Myriads sat in churches propelled by her false system and fed on a doctrine of devils under the guise of the Gospel. As a reminder, gold speaks to our Divine nature in Christ and precious stones speak to our covering of glory in Christ, yet this counterfeit pulled off an outward hoax. Pearls are gems associated with wisdom and her folly is uncovered and destroyed by the unveiling of Christ Jesus, the wisdom of God.

Christ Jesus does an inward work that manifests outwardly. As seen, this counterfeit is opposite. In Christ, the inward man is renewed day by day. It is paramount that people everywhere see the fallacy of a carnal ministry. It perpetuates a system that the Cross destroyed. Anytime one is ready to receive Christ and His fullness and walk in the Spirit, the Power of the Cross begins Its Power within immediately. Skin color and outward vestments do not factor in here because Jesus has been made unto us wisdom, righteousness, sanctification, and redemption. When the Church gets it right the world will take notice!

Many see this counterfeit for what she is. Hallelujah! She is not a queen at all! Not by any means! As Christ is unveiled within His people, all shall see the smoke of her utter destruction. Her musicians, crafts-men, and millstones cannot be heard anymore! No candle will shine in her again, neither will carnal marriages between the unsaved soul and the unregenerate spirit be conducted. All her sorceries have ceased. She can no longer live on the blood of prophets, saints and those slain on earth. The life is in the blood, and the Life is now in Christ the Son. Babylon, the great whore, the counterfeit, self-appointed queen, and every confus-ing, demonic, and false component of her system are fallen!

And they sung a new song, saying, Thou art worthy to take the book, and to open the seals thereof: for thou wast slain, and hast redeemed us to God by thy blood out of every kindred, and tongue, and people, and nation; And hast made us unto our God kings and priests: and we shall reign on the earth.

Revelation 5:9-10

CHAPTER 8

INIQUITY LOCATED

"Thou art the anointed cherub that covers; and I have set thee so: thou
was upon the holy mountain of God; thou hast walked up and
down in the midst of the stones of fire. Thou
was perfect in thy ways from the day that
thou was created, till iniquity was found in thee."

Ezekiel 28:14-15, KJV

INIQUITY, WICKEDNESS, AND UNRIGHTEOUSNESS ARE TERMS THAT REFLECT
the opposite nature of God. Iniquity was found in Adam. Those who
maintain their own righteousness are as filthy rags as confirmed by Isaiah
64:6 which states, "But we are all as an unclean thing, and all our righ-
teousnesses are as filthy rags; and we all do fade as a leaf; and our iniquities,
like the wind, have taken us away." The Righteousness of God is all that
is needed. When the Word says His grace is sufficient it means just that!

There once was a powerful White politician who was once embold-
ened by the support of the Ku Klux Klan, a hate group directed against
Black people, Muslims, Jews, Catholics, foreign-born individuals, and
other groups. This person worked tirelessly to fight racial integration. He
ended up a repentant cripple who had to be pushed around in a wheel-
chair by a Black man. Once a powerful instrument for Mystery Babylon,
he was brought low. For those who say good riddance, the heart must be
changed. The problem did not start or die with that man. In fact, since
his death, it has intensified. Wickedness is spiritual and must be dealt
with on spiritual ground.

Once righteousness begins to work within us, we will take on a different outlook toward racism and all prejudices. Although dangerous, it is at the same time pathetic. People who are being used as pawns of evil and are actually comfortable in so doing are a pathetic sight from the vantage point of the heavenly view. That which exalts itself over others originated as an imagination that exalted itself against the knowledge of Christ. According to 2 Corinthians 10:5 it is to be cast down. Listen again.

Marching and protesting gain much needed attention and ground in shedding light on racial prejudice and other injustices, but people must learn to "cast down" together as they march together. Even God acknowledged the power of people when they become one and have one language (Genesis 11:1). Nothing will be restrained from the Body of Christ when we come together in love. This means all people of the entire spectrum from black to white and all in between. No matter who you are, you are needed as a beautiful part of a grand whole. No empty words but in the power of God's might. Love will force evil out with no means to regain a foothold.

We have been empowered by Christ to do just that if we would only come together as one in Him. It is not complicated. Afterall, the Church should be able to do this because the Supreme Organizer lives within His Church. Oh, how the prejudices of denominationalism, doctrinal differences, and the like pose great hindrances. Nothing will work until we seriously want to see real Kingdom change and our King seated in our midst.

Christ Jesus is the Divine Remedy for restoration and has been made righteousness unto us (First Corinthians 1:30). He loved righteousness and hated iniquity; therefore, God anointed Him with the oil of gladness above His fellows (Hebrews 1:9). See yourselves positioned in Him instead of being a pawn in the world system. To seal the point that man in and of himself is helpless to change racism and other such evils with their far-reaching tentacles forming a labyrinth of systems large and small, let us see precisely what Jesus did through Isaiah's prophecy.

Isaiah 53:1-12, KJV

1 Who hath believed our report? and to whom is the arm of the LORD revealed? 2 For he shall grow up before him as a tender plant, and as a root out of a dry ground: he hath no form nor comeliness; and when we shall see him, there is no beauty that we should desire him. 3 He is despised and rejected of men; a man of sorrows, and acquainted with grief: and we hid as it were our faces from him; he was despised, and we esteemed him not. 4 Surely he hath borne our griefs, and carried our sorrows: yet we did esteem him stricken, smitten of God, and afflicted. 5 But he was wounded for our transgressions, he was bruised for our iniquities: the chastisement of our peace was upon him; and with his stripes we are healed. 6 All we like sheep have gone astray; we have turned every one to his own way; and the LORD hath laid on him the iniquity of us all. 7 He was oppressed, and he was afflicted, yet he opened not his mouth: he is brought as a lamb to the slaughter, and as a sheep before her shearers is dumb, so he openeth not his mouth. 8 He was taken from prison and from judgment: and who shall declare his generation? for he was cut off out of the land of the living: for the transgression of my people was he stricken. 9 And he made his grave with the wicked, and with the rich in his death; because he had done no violence, neither was any deceit in his mouth. 10 Yet it pleased the LORD to bruise him; he hath put him to grief: when thou shalt make his soul an offering for sin, he shall see his seed, he shall prolong his

days, and the pleasure of the LORD shall prosper in his hand. 11 He shall see of the travail of his soul, and shall be satisfied: by his knowledge shall my righteous servant justify many; for he shall bear their iniquities. 12 Therefore will I divide him a portion with the great, and he shall divide the spoil with the strong; because he hath poured out his soul unto death: and he was numbered with the transgressors; and he bare the sin of many, and made intercession for the transgressors.

This is what one sees when a type of King Uzziah is out of the way. After the redeeming power of these verses, what hinders us from allowing the Spirit of Christ to operate in us? Despite the wickedness, He bore it for us all. No one is left out. No prejudice makes one any greater. In the above verses, Jesus tore down racial, sexual, doctrinal, denominational, ministerial, chronological, geographical, educational, financial, and physical prejudices.

Jesus gave mankind a tabula rasa from which His new life may begin and be developed within us. No man has the right to take the place of our Lord. The Preeminence is His alone. As Christ comes through these pages, may we see ourselves as we are in Him. As He is, so are we in this world (1 John 4:17)! We are all spirit beings in Christ and no natural man can take His place regardless of the size of his kingdom. Armed with these truths, how dare one feel inferior to any natural man or woman. We give evil too much space in our minds.

Rejoice not in iniquity, but rejoice in the truth.

1 Corinthians 13:6

It always protects, always trusts, always hopes, always perseveres.

1 Corinthians 13:7

CHAPTER 9

MULTITUDE OF MERCHANDISE

*"By the multitude of thy merchandise they have filled the midst
of thee with violence, and thou hast sinned: therefore I will cast
thee as profane out of the mountain of God: and I will destroy thee, O covering cherub, from the midst of the stones of fire."*
Ezekiel 28:16

THE ASSYRIAN INFLUENCE ON EVERY AREA OF LIFE AS WE KNOW IT IS
palpable. Even so it is part of an even bigger system and we will get to it
directly. Merchandising is the calling card of what the Assyrian speaks to.
Merchandise, trafficking, and trading. Stuff or greed. Assyrian means a
step in connection with success. For many, success is determined by what
one has instead of who he is. The Assyrian was one of the nations in the
Old Covenant that God commanded to be driven out of the land. The
Assyrian and his merchandising skills are prominent in both the world
and church systems. Together they steam power the Great Whore of
Babylon. As this nature evolves, it picks up other dynamic tools such as
media and ultra-modern transportation to parade and convey its wares.
Watch a regular television program and every ten minutes or less this
point will be readily noted. There is presently a rivalry going on to see
who can deliver merchandise the fastest.

Perhaps we can begin to appreciate how the fallen nature is being made an open show. Hopefully, it is more recognizable before it gains further place in the hearts of people. What many perceive as a difficult problem to solve has been reconciled in Christ. What many are waiting on has been here all along. When we see what is feeding the beast, it will be easier to stop contributing to it and starve it. Even more, we will stop fearing it.

Nothing is too hard for God. At one time in history people thought things like slavery in America, the Berlin Wall, Adolf Hitler's regime and the like would be around forever. These examples have resurfaced in other forms and until we deal with the spirit behind it, the next generation will bemoan the same old evil. We are now in a critical state that many believe will never end, but through Christ, we have more control over our destiny than we know.

Back to this thing called merchandising. Merchants! Travelers and traders. Please be reminded that in Mystery Babylon one is a commodity. In that system, souls are no different than cargo. Many nations that are poor in the earth are quite rich in natural resources. God has strategically placed hidden riches to bless His people, but they are often exploited. If people benefitted from their own natural wealth, hunger and displacement would be minimal.

It is not in the fallen nature to do such a deed. Fallen man's idea of trading is not a fair exchange at all but a vehicle of exploitation. People of color suffer the brunt of this misdeed and often their own leaders allow it for personal gain. All is not blamed on a particular group because the spirit is one and the same. Hence this point.

God said the multitude of his merchandising filled the man with violence or oppression. Of course, God is right. Look at what we see. Wars over natural resources. Children malnourished and exploited to get those resources. Ever stop and think why there are children in abject poverty but live in mineral rich countries full of diamonds, silver and gold. The reason is a powerful nation takes from them without giving in return, and there is not a shred of remorse. Oppression is racism's sidekick. Man apart from God is filled with a violent or oppressive nature. It is as natural to him as breathing. It is called the sin nature.

Enter the Lamb of God which taketh the sin of the world. In the Cross, Adam was cast as profane out of the mountain of God and destroyed. The cherubim are beings in union with the mercy seat or lid of the Ark of the Covenant. When Jesus became the propitiation or mercy seat for our sins, Adam was taken out in His Death. The covering cherub was destroyed from the midst of the stones of fire. People just need to hear it by the Spirit.

In the following verses, Isaiah will help see that a phantom is running this world and his prophecy should behoove us to live in the Spirit. For clarity, Lucifer is not a proper name but rather means light bearer. Is that not what Adam was before he fell? Full of light or a being in union with God covered in light! Awake! Arise!

Scripture: Isaiah 14:12-17

12 How art thou fallen from heaven, O Lucifer, son of the morning! how art thou cut down to the ground, which didst weaken the nations! 13 For thou hast said in thine heart, I will ascend into heaven, I will exalt my throne above the stars of God: I will sit also upon the mount of the congregation, in the sides of the north: 14 I will ascend above the heights of the clouds; I will be like the most High. 15 Yet thou shalt be brought down to hell, to the sides of the pit. 16 They that see thee shall narrowly look upon thee,

and consider thee, saying, Is this the man that made the earth to tremble, that did shake kingdoms; 17 That made the world as a wilderness, and destroyed the cities thereof; that opened not the house of his prisoners?

"Is this the man..?" Yes, a mere man and not our Lord. God repeated His displeasure with trafficking in Ezekiel 28:18 by saying, "Thou hast defiled thy sanctuaries by the multitude of thine iniquities, by the iniquity of thy traffic; therefore will I bring forth a fire from the midst of thee, it shall devour thee, and I will bring thee to ashes upon the earth in the sight of all them that behold thee." Unregenerate men are Adam's "sanctuaries" whom he defiled by the iniquity of his trading. God's children are now mansions in the house of the Lord by Christ Jesus.

The consuming fire of God devours Adam's nature, but his destruction can only be seen through eyes opened by the Spirit. Be assured this nature has been conquered in Christ. Ezekiel 28:19 affirms, "All they that know thee among the people shall be astonished at thee: thou shalt be a terror, and never shalt thou be any more." This nature and all its spin have but a season. Many prolong that season because of ignorance of the Power of Redemption. People will either overcome in Christ or struggle in the Babylonish system which disguises itself as high church but is only worldly lust.

He that trusts in his riches shall fall: but the righteous shall flourish as a branch.

Proverbs 11:28

those who trust in their wealth and boast of their great riches?

No one can redeem the life of another or give to God a ransom for them—

the ransom for a life is costly, no payment is ever enough—

Psalm 49:6-8, NIV

CHAPTER 10

HOW JESUS DEALT WITH PREJUDICE

JESUS' EXAMPLE SHOWS HOW LOVE BREAKS DOWN THE BARRIER OF prejudice and its multiple layers. This book could have focused on other aspects of the effects of prejudice such as capitalism which thrives on and is driven by racism or how institutional racism rewards whiteness and systemically punishes color. However, God's love will take the whole mountain down with one blow.

Let us visit an account of an interaction with Jesus and a woman of Samaria from John, Chapter 4:3-29. Having left Judea to return to Galilee, Jesus was impressed to go through Samaria. Clearly, Jesus was not prejudiced against the Samaritans because he used one as an example of goodness and mercy in a parable (Luke 10:29-37). There is a great and powerful advantage to being led of the Spirit of God. Jesus came to a place in Samaria called Sychar near a property given to Joseph by his father Jacob. Jacob's well was there and Jesus sat on the well because He was tired. The Bible explicitly notes that it was the sixth hour of the day which would have been noon in the Jewish tradition when a Samaritan woman approached the well.

Imagine the view if she could have beheld it with eyes of the Spirit. The Well, the Fountain of Life, was sitting on Jacob's well from which she was about to draw water. Breaking through the first layer of prejudice, Jesus asked for a drink of water. His obvious Jewish appearance prompted her to confront him directly for asking of her, an obvious Samaritan, for a drink. The Bible interjected a centuries old fact that the two groups had no dealings with each other.

Jesus then began to deal with a deep-rooted problem from a spiritual manner using the true answer found only in Himself. The Word of God made flesh stated an eternal fact: "If thou knew the gift of God, and who it is that saith to thee, Give me to drink; thou would have asked of him, and he would have given thee living water." This started a life-changing dialog between them. Framing a response from her shallow understanding along with what she could see naturally, she pointed out that He had no means to draw out water from the deep well. That which limits us naturally has no effect on what Jesus can do spiritually!

She then asked from where had He "that living water" He had just referenced. Whether grace provided her a moment of spiritual clarity to ask the question or she was being facetious is unclear. She went on to rationalize her point by asking if He was greater than Jacob, the man who provided the well, drank from it himself and his children and cattle. Prejudice will always justify itself to the best of its ability. Differences are of supreme importance to the issuer.

Jesus responded, "Whosoever drinks of this water shall thirst again: but whosoever drinks of the water that I shall give him shall never thirst; but the water that I shall give him shall be in him a well of water springing up into everlasting life." Yes, in Christ there is a formula for dealing with prejudice that removes the partitions and all the struggle.

She must have wondered how nice it would be to never have to go the well again to draw water and carry the heavy pot home. Such relief evidently piqued her interest. She asked Jesus to give her the water that she would not thirst again, neither come to the well to draw. Without realizing it, she had opened Heaven's Door.

Jesus knew she had to be left on solid ground or the same deep-rooted problem of prejudice would raise its head once He parted ways with her. She had probably met some "nice" Jews before, but the strife remained unchecked and lingered. Is our approach to healing prejudice bringing lasting or temporal results? Remember, as long as there is prejudice, all of us are victims.

Jesus asked the woman to go call her husband and come back. She told him she had no husband, and He responded directly to her answer as correct indeed. He went on to explain aspects of her life to her from a spiritual standpoint. He reminded her of her past five husbands. From this point, she became a representative of the soul.

The soul (the mind, will and emotions), if unsaved, has five husbands which are the physical senses. Apart from Christ, the bond between the individual and each sense is not easily recognizable. It takes an intervention from our Lord to point this fact out. If He is not allowed to do so, when the devil tempts the soul with the lust of the flesh, lust of the eyes and pride of life, she is taken captive. She is also with another husband she is unaware of and his name is "Adam." He is the perpetual phantom husband of any unsaved soul.

After this exchange she perceived Jesus was a prophet. His authority commanded her respect, yet she had to make one last effort at propping up her prejudice beliefs. The Phantom has to maintain his spiritual hold on things or he will fall for sure. She said, " Our fathers worshipped in this mountain; and ye say, that in Jerusalem is the place where men ought to worship." Again, injecting her mind with eternal truth, Jesus told her, "Woman, believe me, the hour cometh, when ye shall neither in this mountain, nor yet at Jerusalem, worship the Father."

There is another dimension that nullifies the personal sides of the issue and centers all things on the rightful place of Christ Himself! Jesus began to teach the woman. True worship in spirit and truth is what God the Father is seeking. God is a Spirit. One can never please Him while uncertain of whom or what they are worshipping. Salvation was of the Jews, and her Savior was right in front of her.

The woman then began to testify of the coming Messiah who would tell them all things. At that time, Jesus formally introduced Himself as the very one on whom she waited. Sometimes we need more one on one interactions in which Christ is given place to minister directly to the heart. The Mediator between God and man is Christ Jesus alone. If the Lord is not ministering through a vessel, that person is the phantom's emissary.

Jesus' disciples came upon the scene at this woman's powerful breakthrough with their prejudices in tow. They marveled that He was talking to a woman but did not inquire as to His reason. When there is no one around to fuel the prejudice, the eternal truth can be solidified as seen when the woman left her natural water pot and went into her city and told the men to come see the Christ.

There is neither Jew nor Gentile, neither slave nor free, nor is there male and female, for you are all one in Christ Jesus.

Galatians 3:28

If you belong to Christ, then you are Abraham's seed, and heirs according to the promise.

Galatians 3:29, NIV

CHAPTER 11

TOLERANCE? SERIOUSLY!

MYSTERY BABYLON STRIKES AGAIN! BABYLON MEANS CONFUSION, AND the whole idea is to flip things around so as to deceive. Tolerance is one of Babylon's responses to God's command of love. Powerless misfit! God commands us to love one another. The love mentioned here is His love, and it is unconditional. Babylon watered love down to a miserable, impotent, hate concealing term called tolerance. We have been accepted in the beloved (Ephesians 1:6), and there is a great gulf between acceptance and tolerance. A command from God is not a suggestion nor an invitation for a replacement with a foolish notion.

No person in this world merely wants tolerance from others. No, it is not even a start let alone a remedy for an evil. Tolerance puts an unspoken but blaring tone that draws attention to differences. Differences demand space and space eventually pushes individuals or groups completely out.

No! Tolerance is not the answer. The ways in which racism and other prejudices have been dealt with is like a child being afraid of the dark because a monster lurks there. No one wants to penetrate the darkness with the Light of Christ. To do so means facing the monster of racism head on. Like David before Goliath, it must be dealt with in the Name and power of our God.

Tolerance creates complexes that acceptance dares to trespass. If all would ask themselves the following questions, it is certain any positive answer would evoke alarm. Yet while unthinkable for many, affirmative responses are a constant way of life for others. Go ahead and quiz yourself.

Who wants to be ignored while others are celebrated and guided to and ensured success? Who wants to be ostracized for absolutely no good reason other than they are in the minority? Who wants to hear social plans made while silently realizing he or she is not seriously included? Who wants to be fodder for degrading jokes? Who wants to be given all the tasks or schedules others neither want nor are required to take? Who wants to be paid less for working harder? Who wants to strive for excellence realizing he or she will be the first to go in a force reduction? Who wants to get passed over several promotions while others less qualified move swiftly up the ladder? Who wants to be the target of the unprofessional law enforcement officer? Who wants to be the professional law enforcement officer who is the target of an unlawful attack? Who wants to drive to the market fearful they may not return home? Who wants to worry for their children all the time due to a hostile society? Who wants to be refused a quality education because of where they are forced live? Who wants to be slighted in the restaurant although his or her money will be mingled without a second thought with those treated respectfully? Who wants to be disenfranchised? Who wants to be jailed long term for minor infractions? Who wants to live in a cycle of poverty? Who wants their family destroyed for no reason? Who wants to be red-zoned? Who wants to feel as though they do not deserve a chance? Who wants to be made to feel as though someone is better than they? Who wants to be leered at as though they do not belong in this world let alone in the same area as some others? Who wants to pay more for poor service? Who wants to be ignored? A list like this is inexhaustible for one who is subjected to racial or any prejudice and tolerance does nothing to whittle it down.

The demoralizing situations above are most real and although expected from the world should not be found in the Church. Are people being placed in certain ministerial positions because they are anointed for them or because of some Babylonish reason that pumps up the fallen man's self-image? Who got ostracized because he or she did not look the part? Churches need to recognize the racial crisis and its impact and minister the Answer instead of being part of the problem.

Legal attempts to deal with racial prejudice continue to fail because man continues to undermine the process and the progress. Laws are made and changed at the whims of those elected. The law of the spirit of life in Christ Jesus will free people from the law of sin and death that moves unabated in this toxic, evil world. If churches begin their next meeting acknowledging the problem of racism and immediately applying the truth of the Gospel by the Power of the Holy Spirit, their people will begin an instant change and embark on a selfless journey that will carry over into workplaces and every other area of society.

Take time and review the following Scriptures and note the last time they were ministered in a concerted manner in your hearing:

John 13:34 A new commandment I give unto you, That ye love one another; as I have loved you, that ye also love one another.

John 13:35 By this shall all men know that ye are my disciples, if ye have love one to another.

John 15:12 This is my commandment, That ye love one another, as I have loved you.

John 15:17 These things I command you, that ye love one another.

Romans 12:10 Be kindly affectioned one to another with brotherly love; in honor preferring   one another;

Romans 13:8 Owe no man anything, but to love one another: for he that loveth another hath fulfilled the law.

Galatians 5:13 For, brethren, ye have been called unto liberty; only use not liberty for an occasion to the flesh, but by love serve one another.

Ephesians 4:2 With all lowliness and meekness, with longsuffering, forbearing one another in love;

1 Thessalonians 3:12 And the Lord make you to increase and abound in love one toward another, and toward all men, even as we do toward you:

1 Thessalonians 4:9 But as touching brotherly love ye need not that I write unto you: for ye yourselves are taught of God to love one another.

Hebrews 10:24 And let us consider one another t to provoke unto love and to good works:

1 Peter 1:22 Seeing ye have purified your souls in obeying the truth through the Spirit unto unfeigned love of the brethren, see that ye love one another with a pure heart fervently:

1 Peter 3:8 Finally, be ye all of one mind, having compassion one of another love as brethren, be pitiful, be courteous:

1 John 3:11 For this is the message that ye heard from the beginning, that we should love one another.

1 John 3:23 And this is his commandment, that we should believe on the name of his Son Jesus Christ, and love one another, as he gave us commandment.

1 John 4:7 Beloved, let us love one another: for love is of God; and everyone that loves is born of God, and knows God.

1 John 4:11 Beloved, if God so loved us, we ought also to love one another.

1 John 4:12 No man hath seen God at any time. If we love one another, God dwelleth in us, and his love is perfected in us.

2 John 1:5 And now I beseech thee, lady, not as though I wrote a new commandment unto thee, but that which we had from the beginning, that we love one another.

Where is tolerance or a policy to adapt to putting up with people and their differences in the above Scriptures concerning God's commands. Nowhere! Decades of the Band-Aid fixes on the mortal wound of racism proved totally ineffective in healing this problem. Love is not forced. It is God in action through His Christ, Head and Body.

Love is patient, love is kind. It does not envy, it does not boast, it is not proud.

1 Corinthians 13:4, NIV

CHAPTER 12

DOES SCRIPTURE SUPPORT TODAY'S RACIST CONCEPTS?

SINCE THERE ARE THOSE WHO BELIEVE THE BIBLE SUPPORTS THEIR HATE, time is given to the topic. With repentance, this false premise is acknowledged as a waste of time, but it will be used rather to prove scripturally that there is no such "animal." Such an attempt to use God's Word to support evil acts committed post Redemption is the spirit of antichrist in its most blasphemous form.

This writing contains many, many Scriptures because few people seriously read or study the Word of God. Many allow tradition to chart their courses thus generation after generation falls dead in the wilderness of darkness outside Christ. Study the Scriptures and allow the Spirit of God to open them and enlighten. Sole reliance of any one private interpretation is unscriptural yet many depend week after week on a pastor or other speaker to feed their hearts and minds. Many have never asked God to fill them with His Spirit. Please ask Him!

The following Scriptures (ESV) are for the reader's edification. There is no support for the use of prejudices or to support racist concepts. All scripture is given by inspiration of God and is profitable for doctrine for reproof, for correction, for instruction in righteousness (2 Timothy 3:16). Scripture is not intended to fuel hatred. If guilty of such, simply repent!

Genesis 1:26-27 Then God said, "Let us make mankind in our image, in our likeness, so that they may rule over the fish in the sea and the birds in the sky, over the livestock and all the wild animals, and over all the creatures that move along the ground." So God created mankind in his own image, in the image of God he created them; male and female he created them.

1 Corinthians 12:13 For we were all baptized by one Spirit so as to form one body—whether Jews or Gentiles, slave or free—and we were all given the one Spirit to drink.

1 John 2:11 But anyone who hates a brother or sister is in the darkness and walks around in the darkness. They do not know where they are going, because the darkness has blinded them.

1 Samuel 16:7 … The LORD does not look at the things people look at. People look at the outward appearance, but the LORD looks at the heart."

1 Timothy 5:21 I charge you, in the sight of God and Christ Jesus and the elect angels, to keep these instructions without partiality, and to do nothing out of favoritism.

Acts 17:26 From one man he made all the nations, that they should inhabit the whole earth; and he marked out their appointed times in history and the boundaries of their lands.

Colossians 3:25 Anyone who does wrong will be repaid for their wrongs, and there is no favoritism.

Ephesians 4:32 Be kind and compassionate to one another, forgiving each other, just as in Christ God forgave you.

Exodus 22:21 Do not mistreat or oppress a foreigner, for you were foreigners in Egypt.

Galatians 3:28 There is neither Jew nor Gentile, neither slave nor free, nor is there male and female, for you are all one in Christ Jesus.

James 2:1 My brothers and sisters, believers in our glorious Lord Jesus Christ must not show favoritism.

John 7:24 Stop judging by mere appearances, but instead judge correctly."

Proverbs 24:23 These also are sayings of the wise: To show partiality in judging is not good:

Revelation 7:9 After this I looked, and there before me was a great multitude that no one could count, from every nation, tribe, people and language, standing before the throne and before the Lamb. They were wearing white robes and were holding palm branches in their hands.

Revelation 14:6 Then I saw another angel flying in midair, and he had the eternal gospel to proclaim to those who live on the earth—to every nation, tribe, language and people.

Romans 2:11 For God does not show favoritism.

Romans 10:12 For there is no difference between Jew and Gentile—the same Lord is Lord of all and richly blesses all who call on him,

Matthew 28:19 Therefore go and make disciples of all nations, baptizing them in the name of the Father and of the Son and of the Holy Spirit,

Philippians 2:3-4 Do nothing out of selfish ambition or vain conceit. Rather, in humility value others above yourselves, not looking to your own interests but each of you to the interests of the others.

Romans 10:12-13 For there is no difference between Jew and Gentile—the same Lord is Lord of all and richly blesses all who call on him, for, "Everyone who calls on the name of the Lord will be saved."

Leviticus 19:33-34 "When a foreigner resides among you in your land, do not mistreat them. The foreigner residing among you must be treated as your native-born. Love them as yourself, for you were foreigners in Egypt. I am the LORD your God.

James 2:8-9 If you really keep the royal law found in Scripture, "Love your neighbor as yourself," you are doing right. But if you show favoritism, you sin and are convicted by the law as lawbreakers.

2 Chronicles 19:7 …for with the LORD our God there is no injustice or partiality or bribery."

Acts 10:34-36 Then Peter began to speak: "I now realize how true it is that God does not show favoritism but accepts from every nation the one who fears him and does what is right. You know the message God sent to the people of Israel, announcing the good news of peace through Jesus Christ, who is Lord of all.

After this I looked, and there before me was a great mul-titude that no one could count, from every nation, tribe, people and language, standing before the throne and before the Lamb. They were wearing white robes and were holding palm branches in their hands.

Revelation 7:9

And they cried out in a loud voice: "Salvation belongs to our God, who sits on the throne, and to the Lamb."

Revelation 7:10, NIV

CHAPTER 13

THE WORDS OF THE OPPRESSOR

They speak vanity every one with his neighbor: [with] flattering lips
[and] with a double heart do they speak.
Psalm 12:2, KJV

SPEECH INDEED BETRAYS A PERSON ESPECIALLY WHEN EVIL ATTEMPTS to feign goodness. If racial and other prejudices are going to be put under our feet, we must be keenly astute when it comes to oppressive communication. This portion of the book is included because often the oppressor's voice is heard in church as much as it is in the world system. Those who are oppressed at home and at church are more likely to be desensitized to it in other arenas such as the workplace and social settings. An inferiority complex can be developed, and the acceptance of oppressive tactics becomes an expected norm.

Oppressive words are often encrypted in otherwise considered nice words. A person devious enough to hide his or her true nature from another can lead a person on with no intention of helping in any way. For instance, two friends worked together and applied for the same job. One was more qualified than the other but was not selected. Of course, that was a crushing blow. The friend who was selected admitted she did not deserve the preferential treatment over her Black friend and honestly confessed to receiving "white privilege." The day after the selection was

announced, the selecting supervisor found it difficult to face the applican
who should have received the position. What was normally a cheerful greet
ing and happy talk from the supervisor turned to a guilt laden sneer. Unfor
tunately, such instances are systemic and frequent.

As our Lord stated in Luke 6:45, "…an evil man out of the evil treasure
of his heart brings forth that which is evil: for out of the abundance of the
heart his mouth speaks." Sadly, the words of the oppressor are prevalent
today and are often under the guise of professional development or worse
yet, ministry. The oppressor's words will lead to some form of death. Be
cautioned to listen intently for the Spirit's Voice in order to discern the se-
ducing words of the oppressor. Often, his or her actions will speak a lot
louder than words.

As seen above in Psalm 12:2, the words of the oppressor have three distinct characteristics. First, they are vanity meaning they are empty. Empty
words lead to mistrust and cannot produce spiritual understanding that
leads to the wisdom of Christ Jesus. The telltale sign of emptiness is that it
is not Christ-centered. In the workplace it manifests in ways such as looking
out for "number one" and only those personally liked. In addition to countless other unfair practices, the focus is on getting ahead or buttressing a racist system. Emptiness will forever place temporal things at the center. It can
only appease the carnal nature concentrating on biological, psychological,
and social areas while leaving a spiritually thirsty heart stranded in dryness.

The second characteristic is the smooth talk of flattering lips. The in-
sincere heart seeks to feel good while dodging accountability. Deep down
one can know change is required to make spiritual progress but instead post-
pones such change. While seeking to feel better about delaying spiritual
progress and deferring to carnal lusts, one is content with a messenger of
flattering lips. Instead of growing up into maturity in Christ, one is content

to be pacified again and again in the fallen state of unregenerate man.

Lastly, the oppressor's words are characterized by double talk. A double heart speaks of a double mind which renders the message unstable. One cannot serve God and mammon, yet one futile attempt after another is made to try it. Such oppressive speech is found in that of the beast described in the Revelation, Chapter 13:11, "And I beheld another beast coming up out of the earth; and he had two horns like a lamb, and he spoke as a dragon." When seen through eyes of the Spirit, the wickedness of the oppressor's double talk is fully exposed. The messenger deceives by trying to appear to represent the Anointed One (horns of a lamb); however, the speech is that of the dragon, the Wicked One (he speaks as a dragon).

Vanity, flattering lips and double talk. Always be aware of what is working through the fallen man's words. Words do not proceed from a pure heart when one is an oppressor. Many people have had their lives devastated by the oppressor whether a slave driver, bully, tyrant, intimidator, dictator or other. Search, consider, and see how that all these mentioned exist only by the power given to them.

God is a defense to all who are oppressed. God is our strength. In the Bible, David said he would sing because God was his defense and the God of his mercy (Psalm 59:17). Upon learning the meaning of defense, one understands readily why David desired to sing unto God while acknowledging Him as his strength.

First, defense means a high place, refuge, secure height or retreat. It represents a stronghold or refuge of God. The meaning intensifies and the term "high" seems less adequate with a closer walk with God. The longer we walk with God the more He reveals the magnitude of our powerful position in Him. Not only are we brought to a high place, but it is one of inaccessible height to our enemies. It is a place in God that is too high for capture. It is a place of safety and security. It is a place of rest and peace.

Lastly, it means to be exalted of God which is far better than self-exaltation. No wonder the Psalms are filled with declarations of confidence such as, "The LORD is my rock, and my fortress, and my deliverer; my God, my strength, in whom I will trust; my buckler, and the horn of my salvation, and my high tower (Psalm 18:2). Not only is our position in God, He is our Refuge where we are safe and secure.

All your children will be taught by the LORD, and great will be their peace.

Isaiah 54:13, NIV

In righteousness shalt thou be established: thou shalt be far from oppression; for thou shalt not fear: and from terror; for it shall not come near thee.

Isaiah 54:14

CHAPTER 14

HOW LONG?

MANY, ESPECIALLY THOSE WHO WANT MICROWAVE RESULTS, MAY THINK the possibility of true change is out of range. With history overloaded with racial injustices, it is difficult to imagine lasting change or real change at all. A dear friend, Lynn Garner, uses a phrase that says, "Changing the kosmos one thought at a time." It is one of the most powerful things if one can grasp it. Our thoughts and deeds are making a kingdom-shaking change to this world system. We have so much more power than we can imagine.

As the pandemic of 2020 is ongoing, there are many things to take note of. First, there is how powerless man is in the face of certain challenges and then there is love's beauty and power expressed in such times. Selflessness that overwhelms the emotions always diminishes the problem. The ability to make a resounding comeback and forge ahead despite setbacks is riveting. Amid this pandemic there are earthquakes, loss and death, unusual weather patterns and destruction, yet people keep moving onward as helpers one to another. Love triumphant! Positive change takes time, yet we all see it can be done.

Scripture tells us the creation waits in eager expectation for the children of God to be revealed. Those words call to mind a before and after picture of the pandemic that was captured of a particular region. What was routinely congested, dusty, dirty, and hazy became clear as crystal. Mankind was temporarily shut down in that region and God's creation could breathe. Clean air with no static of pollution not even man's evil thoughts roaming aimlessly in the atmosphere. A beautiful sight!

That cleansing did not take long at all! However, the beauty of nature is meant to be enjoyed by mankind. There is a groaning and travailing ongoing that is not for the end of man but rather for him to mature and become a son of God. Using this scenario, may each of us purify our new earth environment, speaking of our minds and emotions, by ceasing the choking hatred and pollution of all the prejudices.

Racial prejudice is no different a force affecting mankind than the other calamities. The havoc wreaked is the same. If we can clean up after natural disaster, we can clean up after the spiritual ones through Christ. Notice what happens when people of all backgrounds work together. Many become one and it magnifies the ills of division and all the depravity hidden in it.

Unity is a spiritual principle and that is how positive change results. Psalm 133 compares the beauty of the unity of the brethren with the anointing of the high priest in the Old Covenant. Sobering! Unity and anointing! Spiritually, all are being gathered into One. Many may not realize it, but we are presently being gathered together into the Body of the Living Christ, and we will be delivered from the bondage of corruption into the glorious liberty of the children of God (Romans 8:21).

Finally, brethren, whatsoever things are true, whatsoever things are honest, whatsoever things are just, whatsoever things are pure, whatsoever things are lovely, whatsoever things are of good report; if there be any virtue, and if there be any praise, think on these things.

Philippians 4:8

Be careful for nothing; but in every thing by prayer and supplication with thanksgiving let your requests be made known unto God.

And the peace of God, which passeth all understanding, shall keep your hearts and minds through Christ Jesus.

Philippians 4:6-7, KJV

CHAPTER 15

ARE YOU A HOST?

THE SECOND CHAPTER OF 2 THESSALONIANS IS ANOTHER PLACE IN THE Bible where the depths must be reached and understood if the Church is able to lead God's people triumphantly out of the fallen world system. The chapter begins with a warning of misinformation concerning the coming of the Day of the Lord and how they should not be alarmed. The warning notes that the misinformation may be in the form of a teaching, a prophecy or a letter as if from true apostles.

Notice it does not say when the Day of the Lord comes, but rather focuses on some events that must occur first so one will know when it arrives. Tradition powered by confusion keeps pushing the Lord's Day away in ignorance. The sooner we walk in the power of His Day, the better equipped we will be to overcome the world and its bondages such as racial prejudice.

The message of the Apostle is clear about the sequence of events including rebellion and the revealing and destruction of the man of lawlessness. He is steely in his caution to avoid deception because something must happen first. Verse 3 warns there must come a falling away first. Usually, when people leave a group, the leader quotes this verse. It is mixing apples and oranges so to speak.

This falling away refers to us individually and to the removal of flesh or carnality from our hearts with the laser of the Light of Christ. This is spiritual, beloved, and until this spiritual transaction which is powered by Resurrection Life happens within, we will not recognize that this man who was uncovered throughout the pages of this book is residing within and sitting on the hearts of men and women and children everywhere. This son of perdition makes one his host and his plan is to stay for the life of that host. This lawless man opposes and exalts himself over everything that is called God or is worshipped with the sole purpose of setting himself up in God's temple proclaiming himself to be God.

At the time of the writing of the epistle, the secret power of lawlessness was already at work. The Scriptures warn that this will continue until he is taken out of the way. The Apostle Paul goes on to tell how God would do it. With all things now subsequent to the Cross, it means that God's people have a great personal role in unveiling the man of lawlessness and overthrowing him.

Clearly, the means of overthrow is by the breath of the mouth of the Lord Jesus and his destruction is by the splendor of Jesus' coming or appearing. Man, in his tradition, put these events off to another time when even right now the Church should have Christ on full display for all to see by the Spirit. The breath of His mouth comes through preaching infallibly. The glory and pure brightness of eye-opening and enlightening revelation of Him destroys a lawless gathering. People will not know it is dark until the True Light comes on. Watch the clamor stop instantly when Christ enters in majesty through the "shut doors" and rebukes the darkness.

No wonder no lasting progress has been made to dismantling systemic racial injustices and other evils that work throughout all systems and nations in the world. Where is the breath of the mouth of the Lord? It should be flowing through the mouths of the apostles, prophets, evangelists, pastors and teachers and every believer, but many of them are distracted right now. If not distracted they are waiting on God Who is waiting on them! Mercy!

The lawless one works like Satan does because he is one with Satan. How does Satan work? Just as his name means, he is an adversary or opposing force. The lawless one is a deceiver! Notice all the "power" on display in some churches and in the world yet nothing changes. Fall out in the aisles every week and Satan does not care. Who is becoming a son of God as a result? Not many are being transformed but there are plenty helpers of the lawless one. The lawless one uses fake signs and wonders that are empty lies. Illusions that get church folks to "ooh" and "aah" so they will forget God. This display is not the true power of God. It hurts and harms and makes a spectacle, but it cannot deliver! That is the real sign and wonder that is most obvious yet not seen.

Those who are being deceived are perishing. The reason they are perishing is because they refuse to love the truth and be saved. For this reason, God sends them a powerful delusion so they will believe it. We can either be saved through the truth of God's love or live in unbelief where there is nothing but lying delusion. Before blaming God remember that He does not will that any should perish. Outside Christ one places him- or herself under condemnation where the heart delights in wickedness making him or her a vehicle for lawlessness.

This is how the lawless one moves unimpeded from generation to generation. Think of all the governments he has formed. All the positions he has held such as chancellor, chief executive, chief minister, chairman, first minister, president, bishop, pope, pastor, entire council, and so on. All the laws and policies he has written to support his kingdom. All the schools formed and fully equipped with his materials, equipment, and instructors. All the religions, edifices, and denominations. All the wars, bloodshed, capitalism, and their cyclical patterns. All the murders. All the desecration to the earth and its inhabitants. Think not that all his doings can be captured here or want to be. How he has exalted himself! The lawless one is not our God! Mankind is not meant to be a host for the lawless one but rather a temple of God.

May every hearing heart be dedicated to a forever yes to the true and living God. May each be an instrument of righteousness for His Name sake. May each dispense life, healing, love, peace, joy, and tranquility by Christ Jesus everywhere he or she goes and may each enjoy the same. May great grace, the blessings of God by Jesus Christ, and the sweet communion of His Holy Spirit be yours always in the Name of Jesus! Amen.

If ye keep my commandments, ye shall abide in my love; even as I have kept my Father's commandments, and abide in his love. These things have I spoken unto you, that my joy might remain in you, and that your joy might be full.

John 15:10-11

Jesus answered him, "If anyone loves me, he will keep my word, and my Father will love him, and we will come to him and make our home with him.

John 14:23

CONCLUSION

PRAYERFULLY, IT IS WELL NOTED THAT A SPIRITUAL FORCE IS BEHIND RACISM and all other prejudices. The Church in many ways has flat out shirked Her duties in informing, empowering, and taking care of God's people when it comes to dealing with prejudices. If leaders pushed the spiritual enlightenment of the Redemptive Work of Jesus Christ our Lord instead of their personal agendas and Biblically unsupported religious rituals and requirements, people would thrive. Being spiritually sound impacts every other area of life. Life in our new nature in Christ overcomes the ways of the world.

If only all would familiarize themselves with the "know ye nots" of the New Covenant! We need perfect clarity of Christ, the Light of the world and that which is antichrist or opposes Him. There is a gigantic identity crisis in the Church. Many are misled. Most are always inundated with the problem but never ever given an inkling of the correct Answer.

Evil has a mesmerizing effect that needs the immediate counteraction of good. Evil keeps gaining ground because few are equipped with good which is God's power. Notice how mobs form so easily. People jump into the fray without knowing why in many cases. When the dust settles, there is nothing left but more of the Adamic residue.

Social movements can be quite powerful and often result in change. There is one problem with doing it man's way. History proves such change cloaks a sleeping dragon that will awake again at some point. Church, it is time to allow the Kingdom of God to go beyond man's attempt at change and bring in a whole New Order in Christ Jesus!

For a quick informative course of our limitless power in Christ, let us draw from the first epistle to the Corinthians which contains what we will call the "KNOW YE NOTS." 1 Corinthians 3:16 (KJV) is quoted for the reader's edification:

"Know ye not that ye are the temple of God, and that the Spirit of God dwelleth in you?" 1 Corinthians 6:19, reinforces this spiritual truth with another "know ye not." "What? Know ye not that your body is the temple of the Holy Ghost which is in you, which ye have of God, and ye are not your own?" It is as though the Holy Spirit knew it would seem too good to be true, but we know God cannot lie!

It is hoped that one can see believers are not just noses to be counted in a meeting place. We are the temple of the Lord. Christ Jesus is the High Priest of the temple that we are. He ministers out of an Endless Life, His Resurrection Life. There is no darkness at all in Him and that includes racial and other prejudices. Therefore, one who truly lives in Him has no prejudice in himself. When racism is encountered, recognize the fake glory for what it is and respond in Christ and not in kind.

To steady us on we will focus on a few more "know ye nots." 1 Corinthians 6:9 states, "Know ye not that the unrighteous shall not inherit the kingdom of God...?" Unrighteousness and fake glory are one and the same. There is a place the buzzard does not know, and that place is in the Kingdom of God. Evil cannot enter therein. On the other hand, the righteous can effect change through our God.

Continuing, 1 Corinthians 6:15 provides more blessed assurance as follows: "Know ye not that your bodies are the members of Christ...?" As members of Christ, we are not to be made the members of the harlot system! God forbids it! Come out of her (Revelation 18:4)! Her engines constantly churn out the evil that upholds racism and other prejudices.

In closing, 2 Corinthians 13:5 says "Know ye not your own selves, how that Jesus Christ is in you, except ye be reprobates?" Did you just note Jesus' location pointed out in the last sentence or do you need to read it again? He is in us so now we can stop sky-watching and allow His Spirit to unveil Him from within us! We cannot be friends with the world and with God

Beloved, let us love God and one another!
James 4:4

...Behold, I make all things new...

Revelation 21:5

ABOUT THE AUTHOR

Carolyn P. Bynum is the founder and pastor of Restoration Christian Ministries Center, Sierra Vista, Arizona. She is an anointed teacher sent to the Body of Christ. She has been ministering for more than two decades. Her audio and video ministries are available globally. Her local radio outreach has blessed the local community and outlying areas for more than 25 years. Pastor Bynum is also a musician, lyricist, and arranger who has written numerous praise and worship songs. She served 21 years of honorable active military service in the US Army and retired as a Chief Warrant Officer Three with numerous decorations, commendations and citations from both and war and peacetime. She has a Bachelor's Degree in Behavioral Science from Western International University and a Master's Degree in Counseling from Chapman University. Pastor Bynum wants the world to know that like the Apostle Paul, the Gospel she preaches is not of man neither was she taught it by man, but it pleased God to reveal His Son, Jesus Christ, in her. Pastor Bynum and her husband, Bishop Paul E. Bynum, Sr. have two sons and four grandchildren.

MORE EXCITING TITLES FROM THE AUTHOR

The greatest hindrance to achieving spiritual maturity in Christ is the mixture of law and grace. The Apostle Paul was emphatic to the Church at Galatia and so is this author to the Church today, God's grace must not be frustrated. Righteousness did not come by the Law but by grace, and our Lord did not die in vain. Deeply rooted in tradition is the faulty reasoning that salvation may be earned. The telltale signs are prevalent through the abundance of activities paraded as "ministry." Spiritual clarity and godly sincerity are compromised by fleshly wisdom. Consequently, the minds of many are corrupted from the simplicity that is in Christ.

Sons of God are awakening all over the world to this travesty and are turning with whole hearts to our Heavenly Father as spoken by the Prophet Jeremiah. God will have a People unto Himself and all will know that He is our God and we are His People. Our lives will shockingly contrast that which is profane. The Fire of God has ignited revelation of His love and grace within the hearts of His sons, and we shall walk in understanding of what it means for Jesus Christ to be all in all. Grace and truth, which came by Him, will see to it! The true ministry given by our Lord is to evidently set forth the Gospel of the grace of God. Let us keep it pure this time and go on to perfection in Him!

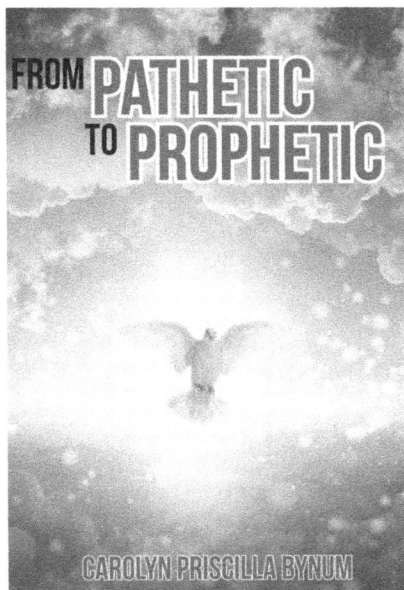

Man has attempted to explain and manipulate the infinite wisdom of God. The Church is suffering the consequences of this pathetic notion. Prophetic ministry has been relegated by many as predictive. Those glued to events and dates are reminded that God has spoken by His Son, and there is a ministry in the earth today divinely enabled to give the spiritual interpretation of all He said. God's purpose for prophetic ministry is much higher and the time of His purpose is right now. We must be keenly aware that only the Holy Spirit is able to unveil the riches in Christ.

1 Corinthians 2:11 (NIV) states, "For who knows a person's thoughts except their own spirit within them? In the same way no one knows the thoughts of God except the Spirit of God." Man pitiably strives to interpret God's wisdom apart from His Spirit. Christ is the power and wisdom of God! The testimony of Jesus is the spirit of prophecy (Revelation 19:10). The Prophet is the Lord Himself. All things are spiritual at this point. Simply knowing what the Word says is not prophetic ministry. As ministers of righteousness our lives must be indistinguishable from true prophetic ministry.

About the Publisher

Let *Life to Legacy* bring your story to literary life! We offer the following publishing services: manuscript development, editing, transcription services, ghost-writing, cover design, copyright services, ISBN assignment, worldwide distribution, and eBook conversion.

We make the publishing process easy. Throughout production, we keep the author informed every step of the way. Even if you do not have a manuscript, that's not a problem for us. We can ghost-write your book from audio recordings or legible handwritten documents. Whether print-on-demand or trade publishing, we have packages to meet your publishing needs. At *Life to Legacy*, we take the stress out of becoming a published author.

Unlike other *so-called* publishers, we do more than just print books. Our books and eBooks are distributed to book buyers, distributors, and online retailers throughout the world – this is real publishing! Call us today for a free quote.

Please visit our website
www.Life2Legacy.com

or call us
877-267-7477

Send email inquiries
Life2Legacybooks@att.net